Emusoi

Maasai girls tell their stories

Macmillan Aidan ltd
323 Regent Estate
Next to mission Mikocheni Hospital, PO BOX 75773
Dar Es Salaam, Tanzania
A division of Macmillan Publishers Limited
Companies and representative throughout the world

www.macmillan-africa.com

ISBN 978-9-987-37352-9

Author:
  Kasia Parham

Stories by:
  Anna, Neema, Esupat, Sister Mary, Linda, Elizabeth, Sifa and Naha

Editor:
  Mike Hollow

Illustrations:
  Emmanuel from the Dogodogo Centre

Typesetting:
  Tek-Art, Crawley Down, West Sussex

Publishing and printing funded by DfID

Printed and bound in Malaysia
2012   2011   2010
10 9 8 7 6 5 4 3 2

Foreword by Gareth Thomas

I was delighted to be asked to write the foreword for this inspiring book. I had the pleasure of meeting some of the girls from the Emusoi Centre during a visit to Tanzania in December 2008. This book tells the stories of Anna and six Maasai girls and the challenges they faced within their families and communities as they struggled to access education.

Fortunately, because of the determination of these girls and the hard work done by the Emusoi Centre, all six of them are continuing their education. Linda has begun medical studies and aims to practise back in her own Maasai community. Naha and Sifa have worked at the Emusoi Centre in between studies and continue to encourage girls from their villages to go to school. Elizabeth and Esupat have now begun school with the knowledge that their story has been heard.

These young women are representative of the difficulties faced by many across Africa and the developing world. It remains a challenge for many girls to get an education and fulfil their potential. These girls' stories show us what is possible.

The United Kingdom's Department for International Development – where I am a minister – believes that education is a right, not a privilege. Investing in education for girls has a positive impact on the wider society by boosting family incomes, contributing to better health and nutrition, and producing a skilled workforce. Educating girls is one of the most important investments any country can make in its own future. I wish Emusoi every success in its important work.

Introduction by Tunu Bwegambile

Emusoi is a precious and important social document.

On one level, the stories teach us about an important part of Tanzanian culture. What better way to learn about life in a traditional Maasai *boma* than by listening to someone who lives there? The illustrations are a powerful addition because they are not created by someone sitting in a studio on the other side of the world, but by a young Tanzanian artist who grew up with the colours and textures of Maasai culture all around him.

The *Emusoi* stories are also a testimony to the vision, courage and determination of a group of exceptional young women. Each one realized the importance of going to school – not only for herself, but also for the future survival of her family and community. Coming from a culture where formal education of females was perceived as a threat, the Emusoi girls had to fight for their schooling. Even when their struggle led to division and heartbreak within families and communities, they refused to give up.

On a deeper level, the book offers a unique insight into the dilemma facing the Maasai today: the tension between tradition and progress, between preserving the past and adapting for the future. The Maasai are an endangered people. If they do not adapt to the modern world, their culture will die. Adapt too far, and their culture will die anyway. The Emusoi girls are at the very centre of the dilemma. They are torn between their conviction that the survival of their people depends on them going to school and their deep loyalty to a culture that does not traditionally have formal education.

As a secondary school teacher, and a Tanzanian woman from the Wakerewe tribe, I can identify with both sides of the dilemma. As a teacher, I believe in the value of a good formal education for girls as well as boys. As the daughter of a Mkerewe chief, I fear that a new generation of Maasai, with no real understanding of the past, will abandon the rich and precious heritage that their ancestors worked so hard to preserve for them.

This heritage stretches back many hundreds of years. Historians believe that the Maasai came to East Africa from the Nile Valley as long ago as the fifteenth

century. They live mainly in rural parts of northern Tanzania and southern Kenya, but, as the *Emusoi* stories show, some of the Maasai are now migrating to urban areas in search of employment.

Like the other 120 tribes in Tanzania, the Maasai have their own particular value systems, traditions, language, customs and food. Each member of every Maasai clan has his or her own particular role, according to age and gender. The male elders are responsible for teaching the young men to become warriors. The women live in polygamous families in which all the extended family members are raised as a tight family unit, helping and supporting each other in times of need. The women look after the home, caring for the children and animals.

Something that many people – including some Tanzanians – do not understand is that the Maasai are not farmers. They do not settle in one place and cultivate the land. Traditionally, the Maasai are pastoralists. They interact with the land in a sustainable way by migrating with their cattle.

History shows that this pastoralist way of life has not always been easy. British colonialism gave priority to wildlife and removed the Maasai from their land in order to create a tourist industry. After independence, both the Tanzanian and Kenyan governments banned two Maasai rites of passage: female circumcision and the killing of male lions by Maasai warriors. More recently, the growth in the Tanzanian tourist industry has resulted in some Maasai turning to new ways to earn a living that take them away from their cultural traditions. And as the *Emusoi* stories show, pastoralism is getting harder.

Traditional people adapt more readily to changes that come gradually, and from *within,* than to changes made by outsiders. When external forces impose their own understanding – in the name of "progress" but without any real grasp of the people's concerns, values, traditions and ideas – the culture is thrown into confusion. In the struggle to survive, its only defence is resistance to change. The *Emusoi* stories record an important change in the Maasai perception of girls' education. Even though this came gradually, and from the Maasai girls themselves, it is still a painful process for the whole community. It is also a beautiful illustration of how one particular group within the Maasai tribe can play a role in the tribe's survival.

The other day, one of my young students, Michaelis Revmatas, made a powerful and insightful observation. Quoting an old African proverb, "It takes a village to raise a child," he said that the future survival of the Maasai – and indeed of any traditional community – depends on the diversity of its members. Just as there must be warriors to defend the villages from intruders, hunters to feed the communities, elders to keep the culture strong and significant by preserving and explaining the past, and caretakers to nurture the extended families and animals, so too there must be "visionaries" like the Emusoi girls to think and see beyond their parents and grandparents and to try to make sense of an ever-changing and confusing world.

Diversity, by its very nature, often leads to tension and heartache. There can rarely be growth without pain. But so long as the common goal remains the survival of the community, each group within the village can play its special part in creating a safe future for the new generation.

I would like to echo Michaelis' sentiments with another proverb, "*Msingi ni mali.*" This is Kiswahili for "Foundation is wealth" and is the motto of primary education in Tanzania. The stories of the Emusoi girls have many important messages, but perhaps the most significant of all is this: that a group of people cannot move forward unless they know where they have come from and can see where they are going. With the help of their elders, the girls make sense of the past and build upon it. With the help of these exceptional young women, the Maasai community may step more confidently into the future.

Tunu Bwegambile MA (Ed) is the seventh child of Chief Mwinamila Lukumbuzya and Queen Corona Musegena of Ukerewe Island. She is a member of the Wasilanga clan and comes from a long line of strong women who understand that formal education and their African heritage have shaped who they are. Tunu's childhood was filled with rich cultural experiences because her father's career as a Tanzanian diplomat took his family all over the world. She realized that her own culture was of equal value and that its heritage should be preserved in an ever-changing world.

Preface   by Anna

My father was a big *laibon*: that means he was chief of our tribe. He had fourteen wives. My mother was the second. Luckily for us, she was his favourite, so we always had food while he was alive.

He was a good man, handsome and strong. And he was not … how can I say this? He was not like the other fathers. He was different. Okay, he was a chief, so maybe that made him different! But there was something else. He was unusual because he believed in education. He said learning was like investing in the future. He thought school should be for girls as well as for boys: for the future of the Maasai, for the future of Tanzania, for the future of Africa.

Not many Maasai fathers say that, do they? They say, "What's the point in educating my daughter when she is about to leave and become part of someone else's family?" and, "Sending her to school won't increase the number of cows I get for her!" and, "Better keep her at home and make use of her while we can!" and, "If she goes to school, who will look after our cows? ME? What? You think I'm *crazy*?"

My father and mother even thought differently about circumcising me.

That's hard for you to believe, isn't it? You people from developed countries call it "Female Genital Mutilation". You say the Maasai maim and cripple their girls. You say it's wrong.

Well, when the time came for my circumcision, the woman arrived at our *boma* with her special sharp knife. Many of our relatives came to watch. The woman told me to lie on the floor and she instructed some of my aunties to hold my arms and legs. She had hardly even begun to cut me when my mother ran over to her. She took the knife from the woman's hand and shouted at her to stop. My aunties and cousins were shocked. They told my mother to let the woman cut me. But my mother would not change her mind.

The thing that will surprise you is that *even I* tried to tell her, "Let the woman cut me!" I *wanted* to be cut!

I didn't want to be different from my friends. I didn't want my husband to get a bad shock on our first night together. Yes, I was scared of the pain. But at the same time, I wanted so much to bear the traditional and special mark of a grown woman. I wanted to fit in with the other girls of my age.

It was the same thing with the holes in my ears. Look! See this big hole in my left ear? My friend made this for me one day in the forest.

I kept asking my mother for big holes, as big as 200-shilling coins, just like hers and just like my sisters'. But she always said no! I could not understand it. *Why should I be different?* I begged her day after day. But each time, the answer was no.

"Wait a little, Anna," my mother said. "The world is changing so fast. There may come a day when you wish you did not have those holes."

"That day will never come!" I replied.

"How do you know? Can you see the future?"

"Do *you* want to sew up your holes? Tell me!"

"Ssshh, Anna. What I want or do not want is not important now. What is done is done."

"But …"

"Ssshh. What is important is this: it will be easier for you to *make* holes when you are older – if you still want them – than to sew them up if you don't want them any more."

That is why my friend made this hole for me in secret one day in the forest. My mother was very angry when she saw it. And she was even angrier when my ear got infected. Eeeah! You would not believe how much it hurt! For days, I tried my best to hide my pain, but then I got a high fever and my mother had to take me to the hospital.

Do you see this circular brand on my cheek? I did that myself without my mother's permission. I wanted so much to fit in with the other girls in the village that I did not care about how much it hurt or about how angry my mother would be.

You want to know if I regret all these things now?

I will give you the same answer as my mother. It is not important now. What is done is done.

While my father was alive, I went to school – even secondary school! But it was only when my father died that I realized how lucky I was. As soon as my brother became head of our family, he sold me to his best friend. My mother and I could not stand up to him on our own, so we asked our parish priest to support me. It was a lot to ask of anyone in this community, but he agreed.

The priest took me to Emusoi and asked Sister Mary if she needed an assistant. She said yes, and I have been here ever since.

I am married now. My husband and I live at the centre with our three children. I work at Emusoi full-time, helping Sister Mary with the day-to-day running of the pre-secondary programme as well as administration of the sponsorship scheme.

I believe passionately in the work we do here. I was so lucky. My parents were visionaries. Don't get me wrong. Don't think they turned their backs on the Maasai tradition. They would never do that, because they treasured it; they really did. But they also knew that the best way to protect it was to allow it to adapt to life in the "modern" world.

That is why they taught me the value of education for myself and for my community. They helped me to see my value, but not in terms of how many cows I would fetch as a bride price! They helped me to recognize my personal qualities and not to waste them. That's why they encouraged me to make the most of my gifts, not just for me, not just for my family, but for all the Maasai.

The girls who come to Emusoi have not been so lucky and I want to help them. Many defy their parents – especially their fathers – by being here. Sometimes the fathers turn up at the gates and demand to take their daughters home. Don't

worry, they can't get in, because the gates are locked and the *askari* won't let them enter. One of my hardest jobs is to meet them face to face and to persuade them to leave peacefully. It can be very frightening, especially when they have been drinking. Usually, they bring a crowd of warrior friends for support. They get angry with me and rattle the gates, waving their *rungu* and shouting.

But I stand firm. I don't let them in. After all, my father was a chief. Remember?

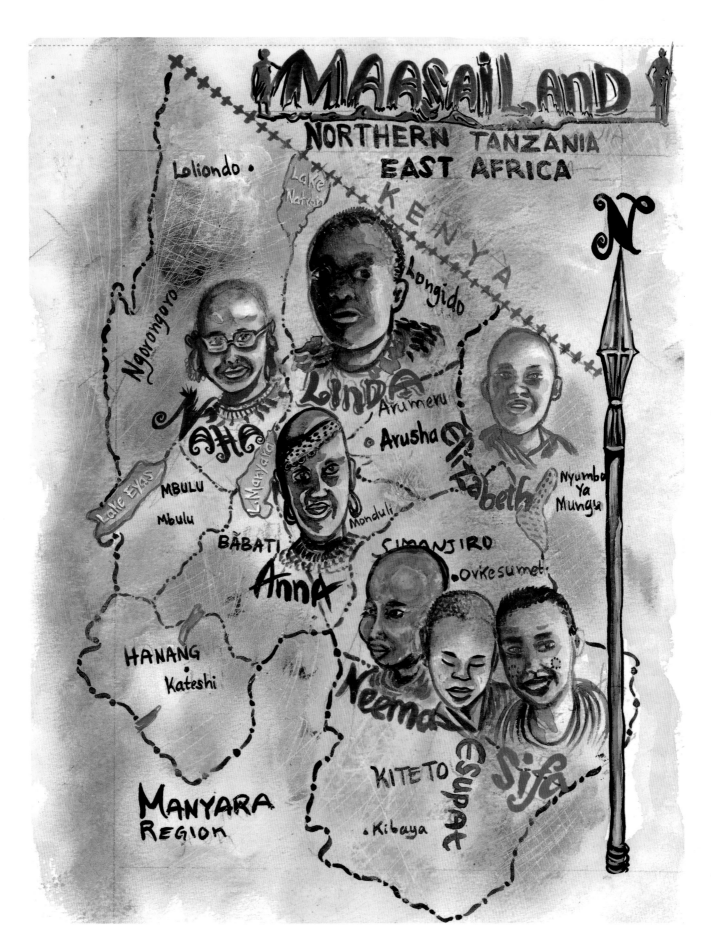

Neema

I was twelve years old when my father sold me.
He did not tell me
what he was doing.
He did not tell
my mother.
He just did it.

The first I knew was when a big car arrived at our *boma*. It just came from nowhere, dropped from the sky.

It was the day after I finished primary school. My mother and I were inside the *manyatta*, preparing *ugali* with milk. Suddenly, we heard, what? The roar of a car engine and the noise of many people, shouting and laughing and singing.

I peeked through a gap in the wall and saw a cream-coloured Land Rover packed full of bottles of beer. I ran to put on my sandals, but my mother held my good arm and pulled me back.

"Don't go outside, Neema!" she whispered.

"Why?" I asked. I tried to break free from her. I did not want to miss the fun.

Then I noticed my mother's eyes. They seemed bigger and darker than usual. They were the same eyes she had when my father was beating her or when I was in hospital with my bad arm. They were eyes full of fear. Suddenly, I was afraid.

"I prayed this day would not come," she said, "but it has. This car must take you away."

I stared at her. I did not understand.

My mother went on. "You are worth more than this, Neema. More than a few bottles of beer."

That was when I realized what was happening.

Then I noticed my mother's eyes. They seemed bigger and darker than usual … They were eyes full of fear. Suddenly, I was afraid.

My father had chosen a husband for me. My fiancé was here, in our *boma*.

That beer was my "bride price". Those people were there to watch and to celebrate. That car would take me away.

I ran to my mother and wrapped my arms round her. I buried my face in the cloth of her purple *rubega*. It smelled of smoke from the fire. It smelled of home. I wanted to ask her not to let me go but I could not find the words. I was shaking all over. Like what? Like a frightened animal.

"Quick!" she whispered. "We will get away. Fetch your *rubega*! Leave your sandals. There is no time. Come!" She took my hand and pulled me through the back doorway. There was no-one around. They were all busy looking at that car on the other side of the house. We climbed over the fence and ran into the forest.

"Don't look back!" said my mother. She was breathing fast. "Keep running!" My bare feet hurt. The ground was rough and covered with spiky acacia. I stepped on something sharp. I stumbled. My good hand was wet with sweat and slipped from my mother's palm. I fell.

I ran to my mother … I wanted to ask her not to let me go but I could not find the words. I was shaking all over … Like a frightened animal.

We kept on walking, mile after mile… Maybe we were walking to the end of the earth.

"Get up, Neema! Quick! We can't stop now!"

"I have a thorn in my foot!" I cried.

"Get up! Get up! Do you want them to catch us?"

I struggled to my feet and on we ran, on and on, through the forest. The pain in my foot was like fire.

It was only when night came that my mother slowed down. But she did not rest. We kept on walking, mile after mile.

Sometimes, she stopped and listened to check that no-one was following. Otherwise, we kept on walking through the darkness. Maybe we were walking to the end of the earth.

It was still dark when we reached my uncle's house. "Pray that he is there, Neema," whispered my mother. My uncle was a priest. Sometimes he was called out in the night to visit sick people. But God was listening. At that moment, my uncle appeared. He wore only a *kanga*. He was rubbing his eyes.

"They want Neema," said my mother.

"So soon!" my uncle replied. "Quickly, get in my car. Let me put on my clothes. We will go straight to Emusoi."

* * * * * *

Before dawn, my mother returned home. I did not want her to go. I was afraid: not for myself, but for her, because I knew what was going to happen to her.

My father was angry. Very angry. More angry than you can imagine.

It is hard
for me to think about this.
It is hard
for me to talk about it.
But I must try.
If I don't tell
people what happened,
no-one will ever know
about her:
my lioness mother.
And about how
she suffered for me
and for girls like me.
Listen!
I must speak.
You must hear
what she did to help me.

They told me that when my mother returned home, my father punished her. He had often used his *rungu* club to hit her, but this time was different. It went on for a whole day. On and on and on he beat her. He beat her until, what? Until every part of her was bleeding.

In the evening, he took her to the hospital. They bandaged every piece of her bruised body. Her lips were so swollen that she could not speak. Her ribs were broken and she could not move. She was in pain for many weeks.

Will she leave him? No. Why? She is used to him. She knows him and she accepts him. Is that love? Of course it's love! Don't you see it? Love for him. Love for me and my brothers and sisters. Love for our people. Love for our way of life.

Years ago,
my mother and father made a contract.
My mother made a promise
that she would never break.
But she said
I did not
have to make
the same promise
yet.

(There was something
important
I had to do
at Emusoi
first.)

They bandaged every piece of her bruised body. Her lips were so swollen that she could not speak. Her ribs were broken and she could not move. She was in pain for many weeks.

Things are better now. My father is beginning to understand why my mother wanted me to go to secondary school. He is beginning to see that our way of life will not survive unless we change.

They said my father got four cows for me. After I ran away, he could not give them back because he had already sold them and spent the money. There is still a problem over those cows. The two families still fight about it.

For that reason, it was many months before I dared to go home. My mother visited me whenever she could and my uncle gave me news of my family. I was afraid of that cream-coloured Land Rover turning up again. I was afraid to face my father.

But things are better now. My father is beginning to understand why my mother wanted me to go to secondary school. He is beginning to see that our way of life will not survive unless we change. I don't mean we have to change completely. I don't mean we have to give up our traditions and our culture. I mean, what? I mean changing the way we look at things and the way we understand them. I mean *learning*.

If I can read and write, I understand things better. I understand laws and rights that protect our people and our land. My understanding gives me the confidence to speak out when laws are broken and

rights are denied. And if people don't listen? Then my learning gives me confidence to shout louder! It gives me a way to defend myself and my people. My father sees that now. He sees that we must change if we are to survive. But we only change if we have learning.

He does not want learning for himself. He likes to relax! But he is happy for me to learn. The last time I went home, he was sitting having drinks with his friends and he introduced me as his "*mzungu* daughter". It was not an insult. It was a compliment. For him, *mzungu* means, what? Educated.

> When I finish my education, I will bring my learning back to my *boma*. I will come back as a doctor … I will bring a good hospital to my people.

I think my father accepts my education because he knows I will not use it to get away from my people. Why do you think I will do that? Will I walk over my mother's broken, bleeding body to escape from my homeland? No. One day I will go back home and give my mother a rest. See my left hand? It was burned in a fire when I was five years old. For many months, my mother carried me on her back, mile after mile, from hospital to hospital, until she could find a doctor with enough learning to make it better.

When I finish my education, I will bring my learning back to my *boma*. I will come back as a doctor. I will help other children with burns. I will bring a good hospital to my people and there will be no need for them to walk anywhere.

Is my fiancé still waiting
for me?
I pray to God, no.
He is not
beautiful.
His nose is too wide.
He has a squint.
His face
is
round.
Like a big, flat basket.
I do not mind that his clothes are old!
But they are not tidy.
Or even very clean.

Esupat

I come from Loiborrsirret, the same village as Neema. My name means "someone gentle and kind" but my father says I am not. He says I am stubborn, like a donkey, because I climbed into Father Karduni's big white Land Cruiser and refused to get down until he took me to Emusoi. I wanted so much to go to school. I could not get there by being gentle. I had to be strong.

When I was young, my father always talked about sending me to secondary school. I would be the first in my family to go. I was very happy because I thought he must love me very much. I liked learning new things and I found school work easy.

When I was young, my father always talked about sending me to secondary school … I was very happy because I thought he must love me very much.

Even when I was in Standard VI, my father did not want me to have an *mbwata*. Sorry, that's when they take out the two front teeth from your lower jaw. It's a traditional way for a Maasai woman to make herself beautiful for a man.

One day, my father was out with the cows and my mother was collecting firewood. I was playing bottle tops with my friends in our *boma* when some women from our village turned up. One of them called out to me, "Esupat! Where is your *mbwata*?"

"I don't have one," I said.

"Why not?" asked the oldest woman, who was carrying a knife.

"My father does not want it," I replied, backing away from her. She caught my arm and dragged me to her. The bottle tops scattered in the dust. Her fingers were hard and wrinkled, as strong as claws. I tried to break free, but she gripped me even tighter and screamed to the other women to hold me down.

Then, using her knife, she cut out my two bottom front teeth. It hurt so much, like a big fire in my mouth. I bled for more than half an hour but I cried for much longer because those were my second teeth.

When my parents returned home, they were very angry. But what could they do? They don't want a fight with that old woman. What's done is done.

But when I started Standard VII, my last year at primary school, my father suddenly

Her fingers were hard and wrinkled, as strong as claws. I tried to break free, but she gripped me even tighter and screamed to the other women to hold me down.

said I had to get circumcised in preparation for marriage. A woman elder from our village came to our *manyatta* and cut me. Everyone crowded round me as I screamed and cried. I could not believe that anything would hurt more than my *mbwata*, but it did. Each time I urinated it felt like knives were slicing

Then last September, during my Standard VII exams, my father announced that I must get married. A man called Tureto had already given him many cows as payment for me.

my insides and I could not sit down to eat. It was better to stand or lie on my side.

I asked my mother if my circumcision meant that my father had changed his mind about me going to secondary school. She said she didn't know. But I needed an answer, so I kept asking her. And she kept saying she didn't know. I was careful not to mention it in front of my father, because I was afraid he would be angry with her and beat her.

Then last September, during my Standard VII exams, my father announced that I must get married. A man called Tureto had already given him many cows as payment for me. We had already sold the cattle and spent the money, so there was no way out.

I knew about Emusoi because I heard stories about it from Neema. I did not want to leave home, but now it seemed like the only way of getting to secondary school.

Tureto was thirty-two years old and I was fourteen. I knew him already and I didn't like him. He was small and thin and blacker than black. He never smiled and I was scared of him. He had not been to secondary school, so he would never understand my wish to go.

I knew about Emusoi because I heard stories about it from Neema. I did not want to leave home, but now it seemed like the only way of getting to secondary school. The priest called Father Karduni had helped Neema to get to Emusoi. He was related to my mother's sister, Ruth, so maybe he would help me too.

Even though Ruth lived nearby, it was not easy to talk to her about Emusoi. Sometimes when we were milking the cows we whispered about it in secret because I was scared of what my father would do to my mother if he found out that her side of the family was helping me defy him.

One day last December, I was on my way to the river to wash clothes. It was very sunny. I decided to pass by Ruth's *manyatta* to ask if I could wash anything for her. When I saw Father Karduni's car parked outside, I knew the time had come for me to go to Emusoi. I ran back to our house and put on my primary school uniform.

On my way back to Ruth's house, I met my mother. She was very surprised. "What are you doing?" she asked. "You finished primary school last September!"

"I am going to Emusoi!" I replied, starting to run. I was afraid the car might leave without me.

My mother ran after me but I was too fast for her. I jumped into the car, put on the seat belt, and locked all the doors. She shouted at me but I could not hear her because all the windows were closed. She banged on the glass. I knew she was begging me to come home. But I wouldn't.

"I'm not leaving this car until I get to Emusoi," I said.

Soon, Father Karduni and Ruth appeared. They persuaded my mother to let me go. I was worried for her, but at the same time I knew that this was my big chance. I had to take it because I might not get another one.

I was crying as the car drove away from my village. I could see my mother's reflection in the wing mirror of the car. She looked so tiny, shivering in her red and blue *shuka* even though the sun was hot. She got smaller and smaller, but I still watched her and prayed that my father would spare her when he found out what I had done.

> I jumped into the car, put on the seat belt, and locked all the doors … "I'm not leaving this car until I get to Emusoi," I said.

Sister Mary adds:

Esupat knew that her father would be very angry. She was so afraid of what he would do to her mother as punishment that she found it difficult to settle down at Emusoi.

Father Karduni decided to go to Loiborrsirret to try to persuade Esupat's father to accept her decision to leave. After four days of heated arguments, Esupat's father finally gave in. With help from Ruth's family, he scraped together Esupat's bride price and returned it to Tureto.

Esupat's father refused to come to Emusoi to give his daughter his formal blessing. So her grandfather – on her mother's side – came instead. The old man laid his hands on Esupat's head and tried to reassure her that her mother was in no danger. This was a great comfort to her, but it is still not safe for her to go home in the school holidays. Like many of the girls who come to Emusoi against their fathers' wishes, she stays here with us.

Linda

There was never any problem between me and my father, because I do not know him. He left my mother to bring up five children – me, my sister and my three brothers – on her own. We are from Tingatinga village in West Kilimanjaro, where my mother is the primary school teacher.

In 2000, my elder brother started secondary school. The following year, I was the only student in my ward to pass my Standard VII exams. I wanted desperately to join my brother. My mother worked hard, but she could not earn enough money to send both of us so she asked our local MP, Michael Lekule, to help us.

Mr Lekule took me to Emusoi, and Sister Mary agreed to take me in and send me to school. After only two days in pre-Form 1, Sister Mary said I was ready for secondary school, so she arranged for me to attend Weruweru as a boarder.

Was I nervous? No! I started at Weruweru on a Monday. By Thursday, I was elected Form 1 Coordinator and I never looked back. You have to remember that I was born in a school! I did not live in a traditional *manyatta*, because my mother always got a teacher's house. My earliest memories are listening to her giving lessons. I knew many things even before I went to school, because I spent all my time with children much older than me.

After only two days in pre-Form 1, Sister Mary said I was ready for secondary school, so she arranged for me to attend Weruweru as a boarder.

I was lucky that I never had to face any opposition from my family. My mother's dearest wish was for me to get a secondary education, so she always supported my decision to come here. Of course she misses me. And I feel bad because she gets tired doing all the chores without me. But she is happy that

She is happy that I've got this chance. She knows I won't abandon her. When I have finished my studies, I will look after her.

I've got this chance. She knows I won't abandon her. When I have finished my studies, I will look after her.

I have just graduated from Loyola High School, where I did Form 5 and 6. I plan to study Medicine at Muhimbili University in Dar es Salaam. Then I will return home to serve my people.

I cry
when I go back to Tingatinga.

Before
I grew tall,
there were trees and grasslands
and fat cattle grazing.

Now there is nothing.
Nothing
but hot
red
dust.
The *morans*
take the cows far away to find pasture.
The women and children
stay home
with nothing.

Nothing.
You don't know what that means, do you?
No meat.
No milk.
No hope.
Nothing.

How will my people survive? My mother taught all my friends, and all my friends' parents, but none of them went beyond primary school. They do not have enough education to stand up for their rights. Their situation gets worse and worse every time I go there. They can barely read or write. They are isolated from other Tanzanians. They do not have the right words to argue with the local authorities about land rights.

How will my people survive? My mother taught all my friends, and all my friends' parents, but none of them went beyond primary school. They do not have enough education to stand up for their rights.

My government cares more about wildlife than about my people. The elephant and the zebra mean big money in Tanzania. They attract *wazungu* tourists and *wazungu* currency, so they count for more than the Maasai. When the elephant tramples on our land, our cows cannot graze there. But instead of helping us to protect our grazing, instead of replacing our lost cows, my government gives us seeds and tells us we must plant! Or start bee-keeping! But there is no market. No technology. Not even any trees. And Maasai are not farmers! Our tradition says that breaking the ground to plant crops is blasphemous. We are herdsmen. We live on cow's milk, cow's blood, goat meat and beef.

> People tell us that if we want to survive, we have to change our traditions … Maybe this is our only option, but we can't do it without help.

People tell us that if we want to survive, we have to change our traditions. We have to adapt to a new diet, a new system of beliefs, a whole new way of living. Maybe this is our only option, but we can't do it without help. Who will help us?

And there's still a part of me that says, "Why should we change? With a bit of help, a bit of understanding, could we not preserve our lands and our way of life and our traditions?"

Sister Mary adds:

Each time I visit Linda's village, the situation gets worse. Last time, there was no water. There had been no rain for months. The river was dry. Linda's mother cried because she could not offer me *chai*. She felt great shame, for Maasai tradition demands that all guests must be welcomed with *chai*.

When I got back to Emusoi that night I could not sleep. I worry about those people all the time. How do they manage? Linda's mother says the children are so weak and hungry they cannot concentrate on their lessons. And with so many of the men away trying to find work in the towns or better grazing for their cattle, the girls are forced to stay home from school to help with the chores. I cannot see how these people will survive when they are so poorly educated. Their entire history and way of life will soon be wiped out. Extinct.

Save the Whale?
Sure.
Save the Rhino?
By all means save the rhino.
But let's not forget humanity.

The Maasai are victims of environmental changes caused by deforestation and increased farming in Maasailand. The land can no longer support a traditional, pastoralist way of life and the Maasai are forced to find other ways of surviving. But it is a slow and difficult process, and they get very little material help from the government. There's a lot of talk in the newspapers about government initiatives and support programmes, but most of the practical help still comes from small independent charities.

As Linda describes, the Maasai who turn to cultivation see their crops trampled by wildlife, or ruined by floods one moment and drought the next. Another girl in Linda's class, Naha, comes from Losimingori, which is a small village on the migration route between Manyara National Park and West Kilimanjaro. Last year, just as the maize was ripening, warthog and porcupine passed through and ate everything. Naha tells me that so far, the villagers have received no compensation.

Elizabeth

I came to Emusoi in June 2007 from Terat, my village in Simanjiro.

The biggest shock was the food. Before I came here, the only food I knew was meat. The only drinks I knew were milk and blood. Suddenly I had to eat *ugali* and beans. And more beans! The beans gave me wind, which made the other girls laugh.

Of course I miss my family and my village, but I love being here because I feel safe with all my friends around me. We are all Maasai, so we understand each other and we have a good time. I live here all the year round because I attend the pre-Form 1 programme. I find the lessons easy, especially maths.

> Of course I miss my family and my village, but I love being here because I feel safe with all my friends around me.

When I am ready for secondary school, Sister Mary will find one for me. It will be hard to leave Emusoi because there will only be a few Maasai girls at my new school. I am worried in case the other girls and boys don't like me. But at least now my Kiswahili is good enough to talk to them. When I came here, I could only speak Maa.

Sister Mary says that when we go to secondary school, we are not on our own. Emusoi still cares for us.

Sister Mary says that when we go to secondary school, we are not on our own. Emusoi still cares for us. We are allowed to come back at the beginning and end of each school term to talk about our progress and to sort out new uniforms. Sister Mary also gives us travel money and anything else we need, like books and toiletries. It is good to meet up with our Emusoi friends who have gone to other schools. We can even discuss our worries with them or with Anna and Sister Mary.

I like it when Linda and Naha and the other Form 6 girls come back to Emusoi. If they are not busy sorting out Sister Mary's computer, they help us with our English. I want to study hard like them. When it is my turn, I want to help other pre-Form 1s, just as they helped me.

I am so happy to be here and every day I thank God for this chance. But I still worry about my mother. Just after I arrived, Uncle Martin, my father's brother, came to Emusoi to tell me that my father was so angry about me coming here, he beat my mother badly and broke her wrist. This was nothing new. When I was growing up, my father always blamed my mother when things went wrong. He beat her as punishment. But this time, Uncle Martin felt responsible because he was the one who brought me to

Emusoi. He works for a charity in Arusha and he understands the importance of education. But he knows how hard it is for my father to accept my decision. My father was counting on my bride price to feed his family. If I go to secondary school, he loses the cows he could have got for me.

When I was only thirteen, and still in Standard V, my father

> My father did not say anything about secondary school. I was too scared to mention it in case he got angry and blamed my mother.

promised me to a man called Nino as his second wife. He even accepted many cows from Nino as my bride price. But then, my uncle Martin persuaded him to change his mind. So the cows were returned and the wedding was called off. For a while, I thought I was safe. I thought my father would agree to let me go to secondary school.

I passed my Standard VII exams in November 2007, when I was fifteen. My father did not say anything about secondary school. I was too scared to mention it in case he got angry and blamed my mother. I did not want to ask his permission in case he said no. So I waited.

In January, the new school year started, and still my father said nothing. I carried on with my chores, milking the cows and washing the clothes in the river, but all the time I was thinking about secondary school and wondering how I would ever get there. My mother said our *manyatta* would not be strong enough against the heavy rains that were coming in March, so I helped her to strengthen the walls with fresh cow dung. But every time someone approached our home, my heart started beating faster because I thought it was my father bringing a new fiancé to our *boma*. I could not relax. I could not eat. I thought I would go mad. It was terrible.

I had no-one to talk to. My elder brother understood me because he wanted to go to secondary school too. But he was away with the cows, searching for grazing.

Then one day, during the long rains, I was visiting my uncle Martin's home, and he asked me why I looked so sad. At first, I did not want to tell him because I was afraid of my father. But when he asked if it had something to do with school, I started to cry. He was so nice, so understanding, that soon I was telling him everything. My auntie Ruth was there too. They asked me if I would like to stay with them for a while and attend some extra tuition.

"Don't worry," said my uncle. "We will find a way to help you. It will not be easy, but it is the right thing to do."

"What about my father?" I asked. "And how will my mother manage the chores without me?"

"Don't worry about them, Elizabeth," said my uncle. "We will find a way to help you. It will not be easy, but it is the right thing to do."

So I stayed with my aunt and uncle for a short time. It did not take long to show them that I found school very easy, so they went to Sister Mary to ask if she would accept me at Emusoi. She said yes, so here I am.

My father has not visited me; only my mother. She says things are all right at home, but I still worry about how much work she has to do. And when my father has a bad day, he always says he did the wrong thing to let me come. But slowly, slowly, I think he is beginning to accept that I made the right choice about my life and my future.

Yet every day, I feel sad for my brother. He wants to go to secondary school like me. But he can't. He has to take care of the cows, otherwise the rest of my family will starve.

Sister Mary adds:

Neema, Linda and the other older girls are wonderful role-models for new arrivals like Elizabeth. They show how studying hard at school gets good results. But at the same time, they are not focused purely on themselves and their own achievements. Whenever they return to Emusoi, they take the trouble to spend time with the younger ones, teaching them English, listening to their concerns, or just "hanging out". They know from first-hand experience how hard it is to make that transition from a traditional Maasai village to life in a large urban secondary school. Their experience makes them far more valuable mentors than I, or even Anna, could ever be.

Perhaps one day, one of them will take over from me. This is my dream: to leave Emusoi in the safe and capable hands of a well educated Maasai woman.

Sifa

Do you see these scars on my face? We call them tattoos and they are typical of Maasai. When we are babies, our mothers cut our cheeks with a razor blade. When we cry, the salt in our tears makes the cuts sting, so we learn quickly that it is better not to cry.

I do not have much reason to cry. I have a happy life. I am luckier than most other Maasai girls of my age. Let me tell you why.

In Maa, *sifa* means gift. It's my name because my birthmother gave me to my stepmother as a present. I know what you are thinking: what's lucky about that? For you, my kind of background seems strange

> When we cry, the salt in our tears makes the cuts sting, so we learn quickly that it is better not to cry.

If a woman cannot have children, she brings disgrace on her husband's family. Usually, he leaves her to find another wife. This is what happened to my stepmother.

and sad, but among Maasai people it happens quite a lot. If a woman cannot have children, she brings disgrace on her husband's family. Usually, he leaves her to find another wife. This is what happened to my stepmother. Her husband left her all alone. The other women felt sorry for her because her soul would not live on in her children, so my birthmother gave me to her.

I did not know the truth until I was fifteen years old, when my stepmother explained everything. I already knew my birthmother, but until that day, I thought she was just another woman in our village. I suppose she still is, in a way. I don't feel connected to her in any way.

Was I shocked when I discovered the truth? No.

Sad? Why should I be sad?

My stepmother really is my mother in every possible way except that she did not give birth to me. I love her. I *love* her. I love her so much, it hurts! Please do not call her my stepmother. She is my mother, and it is only because of her that I am at Emusoi.

My mother had no husband and therefore no cows. She had to work hard on our neighbours' *shamba* in return for milk and maize to feed me and the other girls she looked after. She had no money for my secondary school. Every week at the Pentecostal Church she would ask God to help us.

When I graduated from Standard VII, God did not seem ready to answer her prayers. No-one was prepared to help. Not even my mother's brother would assist us. He lives in a town and understands the value of education. His own daughter is at secondary school, but for some reason he did not want me to go. He advised my mother to have me circumcised and to arrange my marriage as soon as possible.

So after Standard VII, I stayed at home. The short rains came, and nothing happened. The long rains came and went, and still nothing. I tried not to lose hope. I tried to concentrate on helping my mother with her work. She kept telling me to be patient and to trust in God's goodness.

Then one day, we heard about a girl called Leah who had just returned to a nearby village from a place called Emusoi.

But as the weeks turned into months, and the months became a whole year, I was almost in despair.

Then one day, we heard about a girl called Leah who had just returned to a nearby village from a place called Emusoi. She was in Form 3 of secondary school, but she became pregnant against her will during a visit to her family. She came home to have her baby, but we heard that she was

I was not afraid, because this was something I wanted more than anything in the world. And Sister Mary was so kind and welcoming, I felt at home immediately.

allowed to return to Emusoi if she could find someone to take care of the baby.

"Emusoi sounds like a good place," said my mother. "Let us go and ask her about it." My mother cannot read Kiswahili, so the only way she finds out about things is by listening to people. We walked to Leah's village and she told us that if I really wanted to go to secondary school, we should travel to Arusha and ask Sister Mary for help. "This is God's answer to my prayer," said my mother.

Our neighbours and relatives got together and collected the money for my two-day journey to Emusoi. I had no luggage. I did not own anything except the clothes I stood up in: two *shuka,* my car-tyre sandals, my *engimeita,* and some little *shanga shanga* that my mother made for me. I was not afraid, because this was something I wanted more than anything in the world. And Sister Mary was so kind and welcoming, I felt at home immediately. The only thing I was afraid of was that I had forgotten all my learning from primary school. But as soon as I started lessons, I remembered everything.

One of the people closest to me, the girl who was my best friend all through primary school, is actually my birth sister. I was very frightened on my first day in Standard 1. Everything was so new and strange and our teacher had terrible red eyes. This other girl saw me crying and she asked me what the matter was. When I told her, she didn't make fun of me. She let me sit next to her and she looked after me. We have been best friends ever since, even though we did not know then that we were sisters. As soon as she was fifteen, she got married. She did not go to secondary school. We were not surprised when we discovered we were sisters. We felt as close as sisters already. And although we have very different lives, we are still that close.

I come from Same district in Kilimanjaro. My primary school, Ruvu Jiungeni, was 26 km away from my village, almost a three-hour walk away. I used to get up every morning at 5 am. My two sisters and I had only milk for breakfast. There was no lunch at school, so we had to carry some milk to school to have in the middle of the day. I left school every day at about 4 pm and reached home at 7 pm, when it was already dark. We always had *ugali* for dinner.

I don't remember feeling hungry at school, but many of my friends talked about being hungry most of the time, especially if they had to walk a long way to get there. Some of them were too weak to play with me and they used to fall asleep in lessons.

What I remember is enjoying every moment of primary school. I loved it from the first day. I was a fast learner so I passed through the grades quickly and I was always young for my year. That's why I was not circumcised when I got to Standard VII. I was too young! I was lucky.

Apart from the scars on my cheeks, I suppose I am not a typical Maasai girl, am I? I am not circumcised. I do not have large holes in my ear lobes. I am not in my village wearing my *shuka* and car-tyre shoes, collecting firewood in the forest with a baby on my back. Instead, here I am at Emusoi, about to graduate from Thomas Secondary School in Pugu and hoping to study Environmental and General Studies at the University of Dar es Salaam.

Even though I am not like the other girls in my village, I still care about our traditions. I care very much. I want to use my education to help my people to survive.

> Even though I am not like the other girls in my village, I still care about our traditions. I care very much. I want to use my education to help my people to survive.

My fiancé feels the same way. Sorry, did I not tell you that I am engaged? His name is Paul Ranga Lais and I have known him since primary school. I always admired him because he was the first person from our village ever to go to secondary school! Now he is a Doctor of Agriculture and Pastoralism and he works in Moshi. He is trying hard to halt the environmental degradation that threatens our livelihood. But the situation is very bad. Actually, it is desperate, and we are both afraid that it is too late. The process has gone too far.

So Paul is not a typical Maasai either. I was not sold to him. We are together because we want to be.

Sister Mary adds:

Sifa talks about arriving at Emusoi with no luggage. It is hard for teenagers in the developed world to understand what it means to have nothing. Many of our girls really do have nothing, and I mean literally *nothing*.

I remember one girl arriving at Emusoi dressed, like Sifa, in the traditional *shuka* and car-tyre sandals. When it was time for her mother to go back to their village, she asked her daughter to take off her clothes and shoes. They belonged to their neighbour in the village and she had to return them. Luckily, we have a uniform at Emusoi – blue and red checked pinafore made from traditional Maasai fabric, white blouse and black school shoes – or the girl would have been left in my office stark naked!

Most of our families are so poor they cannot afford to pay anything towards their daughters' education. But we do encourage them to contribute in some way, because then they put more value on what their daughters receive, and at the same time they retain their dignity.

Twice a year, Sifa's mother brings us a goat. I dread to think how much she has to sacrifice in order to do this, but I would not dream of refusing. Other parents might bring charcoal, or maize flour, or medicinal herbs from the forest. We receive all contributions with gratitude and respect. What might seem small to us is big for a people who have to manage on so little.

Naha

My parents called me Naha because I was born in the rainy season and my name means "rain". In our culture, rain is a good thing. Rain is what God uses to pour his blessings on the earth.

All Maasai believe in God, but the women, not the men, are the ones who pray. They choose a special place outside the village, maybe a big tree, or a mountain, or a great rock.

All Maasai believe in God, but the women, not the men, are the ones who pray.

My father is not like other Maasai men, because he believes strongly in the importance of educating all his children, girls as well as boys.

They say that God is present in this place, this *oreteti*, and they go there to ask him for help or to thank him for something good. One of the ways of thanking him is to spray milk up into the sky and to sing. This makes God happy.

My father has four wives and twenty children. My mother was the first wife, and I was his first child. He is an important person in Losimingori village: a *balozi*, or "ten cell leader". This means that the families from ten other *boma* look to him for leadership. They expect him to speak

up for them when they feel unjustly treated by the authorities in Monduli District. They expect him to set a good example by the way he behaves.

My father is not like other Maasai men, because he believes strongly in the importance of educating all his children, girls as well as boys. When I was five years old, he was away in Namanga selling cattle, but he sent a message home telling my mother it was time to send me to primary school. But I failed the size test. When I stretched my right arm over my head and tried to touch my left ear, it would not reach! This was the sign that I was not yet big enough for school. I had to grow a bit more.

When I started in Standard I, my cousin Nguja took me to school every day. It was a nuisance for her because I was in the first shift, which started at 7 am, and she had to hang around until noon for her own class to begin. There are still shifts in most primary schools, because there are not enough classrooms.

At the beginning, I was very embarrassed because I did not have a smart uniform like the other children. When my father came home after a long time away, he noticed my old clothes and went out to buy me beautiful new ones. I was so proud. I think he must love me very much.

Later on, when I reached Standard IV, my father said that my two front teeth had to come out. I was very upset because I had just started English lessons and I knew the *mbwata* would make some words very difficult to pronounce. I did not want to say "free" instead of "three". My father listened to me and agreed to leave my teeth alone. All my sisters have kept their teeth as well.

Like many Maasai men, my father finds change very difficult. Our traditions mean so much to him and it breaks his heart to watch them slowly disappear. But at the same time, he is not like other men, because he is prepared to listen to another point of view. He is open to a new approach and to consider when change might be necessary. It takes a lot of courage to be like that, especially if it makes you different from your friends and family. I think he is very brave.

When I reached Standard VII, my father wanted me to go to Maasae Girls' Secondary School, which had been started by the Lutheran Church the year before. Two girls from Losimingori were already in Form 1. They were the first people from my village ever to go to secondary school!

Unfortunately, no-one in my village passed Standard VII that year and I had to repeat the year. It was very boring. I found the work too easy. I knew that I was ready for Form 1.

I am not just saying this because I failed, but I have to tell you that there was a lot of cheating surrounding those exams. People were so desperate to get their children to the new secondary school that

We do not have birth certificates or identity cards in Maasailand, so it is difficult to keep track of exactly who is who.

they were prepared to pay bribes to officials to "sell" the identities of the children on the pass list. We do not have birth certificates or identity cards in Maasailand, so it is difficult to keep track of exactly who is who.

People say that the system is now less corrupt, but this kind of thing still happens. We have to do something to stop it. We have to increase the number of good schools so there are enough places for everyone. We have to pay officials properly so they are not tempted by bribes. We have to improve the quality of teaching so that the next generation is better educated and more able to cope with all the changes around us.

We have to improve the quality of teaching so that the next generation is better educated and more able to cope with all the changes around us.

I came to Emusoi in 1999. Sister Mary had just started up a hostel for six Maasai girls who were already in secondary school but were finding it difficult to manage. They could not afford good accommodation and they needed

I already had a fiancé, but I kept hoping that my father would delay my marriage long enough for me to get safely to school.

support because they felt like outsiders, far away from everything they knew. Even their Kiswahili was not very good.

The hostel was in Arusha town (not where Emusoi is now), and soon word spread to our village about the help Sister Mary was giving to Maasai girls. It was July and I was still in my second year of Standard VII. My father was giving up hope that I would ever get to secondary school and was under pressure from his family to arrange my wedding. I already had a fiancé, but I kept hoping that my father would delay my marriage long enough for me to get safely to school.

Then one day, my fiancé turned up at our *boma* to take me away. My mother somehow got a message to Sister Mary, asking her to come quickly and get me. She did! She drove out to my village. My fiancé was very angry. He threatened to put a curse on Emusoi if Sister Mary took me away. My father was afraid and almost changed his mind, but my mother was not scared. She is a strong Christian. "I don't believe in curses!" she said. "Nor do I!" said Sister Mary.

So I left home in Sister Mary's big white Land Cruiser and went to live with her at Emusoi. I joined

Form 1 of St Joseph's High School as a day pupil. After Form 3, I became a boarder. This year, I finished my A-levels at St Mary's Seminary School in Tanga and I hope to go on to university to study accountancy. I want to use my new skill to serve my community. It will give me the power to help Maasai people to set up their own businesses. Many of them can no longer rely on the land to

This year, I finished my A-levels at St Mary's Seminary School in Tanga and I hope to go on to university to study accountancy. I want to use my new skill to serve my community.

provide them with a living. They have to find other ways to survive. Maasai women are very resourceful. I think, with a bit of help, many of them could be good businesswomen.

I feel great pain in my heart when I think of other Maasai girls who are not as lucky as I am. That is why I try to help other girls in my village. Although my father is happy for me to be at Emusoi, he does not like me interfering with other families because it causes division and distress and often, violence. But what can I do? The future of the Maasai depends on the education of the women. What good is it if only a handful of us are educated? Our voices will not be loud enough! No. I have a duty to encourage other girls to follow in my footsteps. If they come and ask me to help them, how can I turn them away when I am here, benefiting so much from what education has to offer me? Tell me, which is the loudest: one voice, ten voices, or two hundred voices? I can't get the government to listen to me on my own. But they can't close their ears to a whole choir.

The future of the Maasai depends on the education of the women. What good is it if only a handful of us are educated? Our voices will not be loud enough!

She was standing by the roadside on her own in the dark for almost two hours, afraid that a hungry lion or an angry buffalo would come to get her.

Three years ago, I was at home in my village when my cousin Maria asked me to help her. Her father, who is my father's brother, had already sold her, but she did not want to get married. She was afraid to come to Emusoi in case her father punished her mother by beating her. She was afraid of what would happen to her brothers and sisters after she left.

I contacted Sister Mary and asked her to send a letter to the village elder, explaining that Maria wanted to attend secondary school and that Emusoi was prepared to meet the cost. To begin with, nothing happened. Then, I was given a letter to deliver to Sister Mary when I returned to Emusoi a few days later. The letter was from the doctor, stating that Maria was pregnant and therefore could not attend school. Maria and I both knew that this was a lie. Her fiancé had paid the doctor to say this.

But what could we do? There was no point in challenging the doctor. No-one would listen. Maria's only chance of getting to school was to run away. A few days later, I was leaving for Emusoi. It was a Wednesday. Maria's brother, who knew about our plan, brought some clothes from their *manyatta* for me to wash. This gave Maria a perfect excuse to come over later. As I handed her the big bundle of clean clothes, I slipped the money for her bus fare into her hand.

That evening, Maria told her mother that she planned to leave home at 4 am the next day. Both of them were very scared because they knew what my uncle would do to her. But she gave Maria her blessing.

When Maria arrived at Emusoi the next day, I was so happy to see her. She told me how scared she had been while waiting for the bus to Mbauda. She was standing by the roadside on her own in the dark for almost two hours, afraid that a hungry lion or an angry buffalo would come to get her. When she got to Arusha, she was even more scared because it was the first time she had ever been to a town.

That Thursday was the longest day of my life. Every moment, I expected my uncle to turn up and demand to take his daughter home. Maria's brother called, as we had arranged, to check that Maria had arrived safely. He said everyone suspected that I had helped Maria to escape, but no-one knew for certain. I begged him not to say where she was and he agreed. Two days later, my father called and asked me whether I had Maria with me. I could not lie. I had to say yes. Well, he went crazy. Completely crazy. Never in my life have I heard such angry words. I cried and cried. How can I explain to him that I care so much about him and I hate to cause him pain, but at the same time I care about my people and I have to help them if I can?

> I wish I could persuade her that she would help not just herself but also her child if she came back.

Maria was at Emusoi for a year. Then her father asked her to go home so that he could give her his blessing. We were all overjoyed. But it was a trick. Somehow, Maria was persuaded to sleep with her fiancé, and she got pregnant. I am not sure what made her do it, but her family probably scared her with talk of superstition and witchcraft. Talk like that is hard to resist.

So Maria married her fiancé. Sister Mary offered to take her back after the birth, so long as she could find someone to take care of the baby. Even her husband agreed. But she has not come. She is still at home. Every time I see her, she just cries and tells me how unhappy she is. I tell her that it is not too late and she can still come back to school. But she hasn't come. I wish I could persuade her that she would help not just herself but also her child if she came back.

I still find it awkward going home, because my father cannot forgive me for helping Maria to run away.

Whenever the subject comes up, we argue. It makes me sad because I love him so much and I want him to be proud of me in front of our village, not ashamed. Maybe one day he will see that all the trouble caused by girls' education is worthwhile. Sister Mary promised me that one day my people will thank me. I don't want their thanks! I just want them to recognize education as the way to survive. I want them to take hold of any chances I can give them.

Only when I have finished my studies, only when I have got all my qualifications, will I be able to make a difference to the lives of my people. Perhaps at last, they will be convinced of the power that education brings.

But it takes a very long time, doesn't it?

And a lot of patience.

And there is so much heartache on the way.

Only when I have finished my studies, only when I have got all my qualifications, will I be able to make a difference to the lives of my people.

Sister Mary adds:

Maria's story shows how the lack of education makes young Maasai women so vulnerable. Maria did not have the confidence to resist pressure from her family and her fiancé, particularly when they frightened her with talk of evil spirits. Naha, on the other hand, has been with us since 1999. Her education gives her the power to stand up for herself and to make her own informed choices about her future.

Naha hopes to study accountancy because she recognizes that the economic empowerment of Maasai women entrepreneurs is crucial to their survival. These days, many of the *morans* are leaving the villages to find work in the towns as *walinzi*. Their salaries are so low that there is not much left to send home to help the family. The women create small businesses grinding *engisugi,* making shoes from car tyres or creating bead artefacts to sell in the markets. But without a good education, or even much Kiswahili, they find it hard to develop their businesses enough to make a decent living.

When the *morans* return from the towns, they bring not only money but also HIV. Without education, Maasai women are vulnerable to infection. They have no real idea what HIV is or how it spreads, and no means of protecting themselves. Few can afford anti-retroviral drugs. The problem is compounded by the Maasai tradition that when an *mgeni* arrives at the *boma*, a woman's husband gives the guest his place in the marital bed and sleeps elsewhere. Many instances of rape, resulting in pregnancy and HIV infection, come from this practice.

I think Naha is very brave to continue helping other girls to follow in her footsteps, despite opposition from her father. Two more of our students, Naipa and Selelo, are now at Emusoi because Naha went to the District Council and organized letters to be sent to the girls' families requesting consent for their entry to secondary school. The people in Naha's village know that she is behind it. It is hard for her to go home and face disapproval of what she is doing, but she still goes. She does not turn her back.

Emusoi Centre

Emusoi means "discovery" or "awareness" in Maa, the language of the Maasai.

The Emusoi Centre provides access to post-primary education for Maasai girls.

The Emusoi Centre for Pastoralist Girls was established by Maryknoll Sister Mary Vertucci in Arusha in response to the lack of opportunities for girls' education in the indigenous pastoralist and hunter-gatherer communities of Tanzania.

Within the Maasai community, only a small percentage of girls finish primary school and even fewer continue through secondary education. Only twenty Maasai women in Tanzania have a first degree and just one has a second. There are fewer than twenty Maasai women primary school teachers, no doctors and only one lawyer – herself an Emusoi graduate.

The centre, which began in 1999 with six students, now supports almost 600 young women in multicultural, multi-tribal secondary schools, vocational training centres, colleges and universities all over Tanzania. Under the management of Emusoi's Director, Sister Mary, a team of teachers and counsellors tracks the progress of each student, providing educational guidance and moral support as well as school fees, uniform, travel expenses and books. Emusoi staff work closely with village elders, churches, NGOs and local government officials to encourage parents in pastoralist communities to give their daughters greater opportunities for education.

In addition, Emusoi houses a residential pre-secondary programme for 80–100 young women. This programme opened in October 2004 in response to an urgent need for a transitional space for young women coming from traditional lifestyles. Here, graduates from Maasai primary schools are prepared academically, socially and psychologically for their secondary education. Older girls, who are at risk of enforced marriage if they return home, work at the centre as teachers' assistants and mentors while they wait for their examination results.

Emusoi staff also prepare students for life in a global community, advising them on how best to use their qualifications for their own benefit and for the sustainable development of their villages.

Ways to send funds to the Emusoi Centre

Funds can be channelled via the Tanzania Development Trust, the charitable arm of the Britain–Tanzania Society, based in the UK.

Cheques: payable to Tanzania Development Trust, sent to Treasurer, 564 Wimborne Road East, Ferndown, Dorset BH22 9NQ (UK).

Bank payments: CAF Bank, sort code 40-52-40, a/c no. 00006990, a/c name Tanzania Development Trust. Payment Reference: Emusoi Centre.

International bank payments: HSBC Bank, Poultry and Princes St Branch, London, UK, Swift Branch ID Code MIDLGB2141W, a/c name CafBank Ltd, a/c no. 72138549, sort code 400530, IBAN no. GB48MIDL40053072138549, Beneficiary: Tanzania Development Trust, Beneficiary a/c no. 00006990. Payment reference: Emusoi Centre.

Gift Aid mandate forms (for UK income tax payers) and Standing Order forms for regular bank payment are available at www.btsociety.org

Cheques from USA:
Cheques can be sent to Maryknoll Sisters, Box 311, Maryknoll, NY 10545-0311, USA. Please make them payable to "Maryknoll Sisters" but they should be designated for Emusoi Centre, c/o Sr Mary Vertucci, Tanzania. Please write "Emusoi Centre" on the memo line of the cheque.

From Tanzania:
1. Tanzanian shillings
Account Name: Maryknoll Sisters – Emusoi Centre
Account Number: 01J1035766100
Branch: CRDB-Meru

2. US dollars
Account Name: Maryknoll Sisters – Meru
Account Number: 02J1035766000
Branch: CRDB-Meru

Contact details for the Emusoi Centre

PO Box 1547

Arusha

Tanzania

Tel: 255-27-2503042

To sponsor an individual Emusoi student, or to receive the bi-annual Emusoi newsletter, write to Sister Mary at emusoi@bol.co.tz or visit www.emusoicentre.co.tz

Glossary of Maa and Kiswahili terms

askari	security guards
balozi	local leader of ten households
boma	settlement enclosing a group of Maasai huts (*manyatta*) belonging to one family; surrounded by a thick fence of thorny acacia branches
chai	tea
emusoi	discovery, awareness
engimeita	traditional necklace
engisugi	powdered tobacco or snuff
kanga	richly coloured, patterned wrap-around clothing, similar to a sarong
laibon	Maasai chief ritual leader and "medicine man"
Maa	language of the Maasai people
manyatta	earthen huts built in a ring within each Maasai *boma*
mbwata	gap left by the removal of two front teeth from Maasai woman's lower jaw
mgeni	guest (pl. *wageni*)
moran	Maasai warrior
mzungu	outsider, foreigner (pl. *wazungu*)
oreteti	holy place where God is present and where Maasai gather for prayer
rubega	set of wrap-around garments (e.g. *shuka, kanga*) knotted over the shoulder like a toga. Maasai women's *rubega* are longer than men's, carefully layered to cover more of their body.
rungu	(pl. *marungu*) wooden club used by Maasai male warriors in warfare and for hunting. They are 18–20 inches long with a heavy ball at one end.
shamba	farm
shanga shanga	jewellery made with small coloured beads
shuka	checked blanket, usually red and purple, which can also be worn
ugali	cornmeal porridge, staple food of Tanzania
walinzi	security guards